Who Is
Bad Bunny?

Who Is
Bad Bunny?

by G. M. Taboas Zayas

illustrated by Andrew Thomson

Penguin Workshop

To Bad Bunny's fans, and all my love
to my friends in Puerto Rico—GMTZ

For Rhia, Cerys, and Esme—AT

PENGUIN WORKSHOP
An imprint of Penguin Random House LLC, New York

First published in the United States of America by Penguin Workshop,
an imprint of Penguin Random House LLC, New York, 2024

Visit us online at penguinrandomhouse.com.

Library of Congress Cataloging-in-Publication Data is available.

Printed in the United States of America

ISBN 9780593754764 (paperback)   10 9 8 7 6 5 4 3 2 1 CJKW
ISBN 9780593754771 (library binding)   10 9 8 7 6 5 4 3 2 1 CJKW

Contents

Who Is Bad Bunny?

On February 5, 2023, Benito Antonio Martínez Ocasio, known throughout the world as Bad Bunny, prepared to perform at the sixty-fifth annual Grammy Awards.

Backstage, performers warmed up and got dressed as plena dancers, a type of music and dance born in Puerto Rico that blends African and Latin American music. Some even wore cabezudos, giant heads made of papier-mâché, representing famous Puerto Rican icons like poet Julia de Burgos, baseball legend Roberto Clemente, singer Tego Calderón, and many more.

Benito opened the event with a burst of tambourines, drums, and the plena dancers moving around him before beginning with "El Apagón," "The Blackout," a song that tackled the ongoing blackouts in Puerto Rico and celebrated his pride as a Puerto Rican. He followed it with "Después de la Playa," "After the Beach," with Dahian el Apechao's Dominican band playing and over forty performers dancing merengue. They moved among celebrities like Jack Harlow, Taylor Swift, and LL Cool J.

For many Bad Bunny fans from Puerto Rico,

the scene depicted the first day of San Sebastián, a festival filled with artisans, music, food, and endless fun. But this night was special for Benito. Not only was his album *Un Verano Sin Ti*, "A Summer Without You," nominated for Best Música Urbana Album and his song "Moscow Mule" nominated for Best Pop Solo Performance, but he made history as the first artist with a Spanish-language album to be nominated for Album of the Year, alongside Harry Styles's album *Harry's House*, Adele's *30*, and Beyoncé's *Renaissance*.

That night, Benito did not win Album of the Year. But he won Best Música Urbana Album. In English and Spanish, he thanked his fans, his friends, and producers, and dedicated the award to Puerto Rico, the birthplace of reggaeton (say: reh-gey-ton), a musical style that combines hip-hop, dancehall reggae, and Caribbean music.

"I made this album with love and passion," he said to the crowd. "And when you do things with love and passion, everything is easier."

CHAPTER 1
Growing Up in Vega Baja, Puerto Rico

Benito Antonio Martínez Ocasio was born in Vega Baja, Puerto Rico, on March 10, 1994. His father, Tito, was a truck driver and his mother, Lysaurie, a schoolteacher. In time, he had two younger brothers, Bysael and Bernie. The family lived in Almirante Sur, a small community nestled between the beach and mountains, just forty minutes away from the capital city of San Juan.

While life wasn't always easy, his parents did their best to provide for their three sons. Their trips to San Juan were special occasions. Benito and his brothers enjoyed visiting music stores there and staring at the music albums and DVDs they displayed.

Bernie and Benito

While many of his classmates saw Benito as the class clown, he always preferred to be at home with his family. He loved playing outside and pretending to be a WWE (World Wrestling Entertainment) wrestler or swimming in the river in Vega Baja. The first time he ever left the island was to visit family in the United States, and his brothers remember how he cried the entire plane ride.

Benito's love of music came at an early age. His parents played different styles of music around the house, from salsa, merengue, and pop ballads to early reggaeton. But no single artist inspired him. Instead, the entire Latine movement—led by giants such as Hector Lavoe, Marc Anthony, Tego Calderón, and many more—fueled Benito's dreams of making music and having people listen to it. For Christmas and Día de los Reyes (Three Kings Day), instead of toys he'd ask for CDs by singers like Marc Anthony, Vico C, and even bolero music (Cuban love songs). He'd listen to each CD until well past midnight, always getting in trouble with his parents for staying up late.

Benito sang in the church choir until he was thirteen. And for his middle school talent show, he sang "Mala Gente," "Bad People," by Colombian rocker Juanes, showing off his strong vocal style, even though he was terrified of performing onstage. He began to learn how to make beats using computer programs like FruityLoops and started freestyling at school. Benito even introduced FruityLoops to his childhood friend Ormani Pérez, who would later become his closest collaborator on his biggest hits.

By high school, Benito's taste in music expanded to experimenting with reggaeton and trap music, a type of rap, creating original music with his friends. His classmates still viewed him as the class clown as he created rhymes on the spot, teasing his friends. But outside of school, Benito took his art more seriously. He was driven by his love of music and support from his friends, who urged him to share his music online.

Even though Benito knew he had the talent, he refused to post any of his original songs just yet. But something began to change in Benito, and in an interview with the online magazine *Fader* he said, "little by little, something was working in my mind," and he knew his friends were right and that he needed to share his talent outside the comfort of his home and school.

CHAPTER 2
The Birth of Bad Bunny

After he graduated high school, Benito attended the University of Puerto Rico at Arecibo, studying audiovisual communications, and worked part-time in an Econo supermarket. Benito failed all his university classes in his first semester except for the ones in his major and mathematics. He was too busy writing lyrics and creating beats and rhythms to make much time for schoolwork.

Thanks to his friends' support, Benito started uploading his first few songs in 2016 to SoundCloud, a music streaming service. He released his songs under the name "Bad Bunny," inspired by a childhood picture of him dressed as the Easter Bunny for school.

His single "Diles," "Tell Them," became a runaway hit, gaining more and more attention online. By the time DJ Luian from Hear This Music record label discovered him, the song had already hit over one million streams!

Now with a record company behind him, Benito got to work, releasing several singles on YouTube and performing anywhere he could. By the end of 2016, his single "Soy Peor," "I'm Worse," a song about breaking up with someone and wondering if it's for the best, hit the Hot Latin Songs chart at number nineteen.

In an interview, Benito said, "[It] confirmed what I already knew. It let me know that I had the talent to achieve something." And, much like his growing fan base, his collaborations expanded to include performances with singers like Ozuna, Karol G, J Balvin, and other artists he would continue to work with many more times during his career.

Benito not only became known for his powerful baritone voice, fun lyrics, and danceable beat but also for his fashion. As Bad Bunny, he performed with manicured hands and brightly colored clothes. His style was unique, a lot like his music, and allowed him to express himself the way he wanted to. He did not define clothes as made for boys or girls but wore whatever made him feel the most confident in that moment.

In 2017, Puerto Rico was struck by Hurricane María. Almost three thousand people were killed and over three hundred thousand homes were destroyed. Benito, now twenty-three years old, had been on tour in South America and was writing his first solo album. Distressed by the news, he flew home to be with his family, who were without power for months. "I would've given anything to have been there in that moment," he said in an interview with *Rolling Stone* magazine.

The hurricane and its aftermath sparked Benito's interest in politics. He was furious because Puerto Ricans had been left without food, water, electricity, and other resources for months that dragged on into years. Benito would later dedicate the song "Estamos Bien," "We're Okay," to the victims of Hurricane María.

CHAPTER 3
X 100PRE

Just before his debut album released, Benito was invited to collaborate with Cardi B and J Balvin for "I Like It," a blend of the boogaloo song "I Like It Like That" by Pete Rodriguez, trap, and salsa. The song blended English and Spanish lyrics. Benito had played with J Balvin before, and they became close friends. Shortly after, he released a single with Drake titled "Mia," "Mine."

On December 24, 2018, Benito released his first solo album, *X 100PRE*. The title is a shortened way of saying *por siempre*, or "forever." The album became a huge international hit. It eventually ranked number forty-one on *Rolling Stone*'s "100 Best Debut Albums of All Time," eleven on the *Billboard* 200, number one on Top Latin Albums and Latin Rhythm Albums, and it won the Latin Grammy award for Best Urban Music Album in 2019. The album included collaborations with Drake, Ricky Martin, Diplo,

and El Alfa. He had released singles for years, and now his album proved he was a superstar who was here to stay. And not long before his album's release, Benito moved on from Hear This Music to a new record label, Rimas Entertainment.

Benito, Bysael, and Bernie Martínez Ocasio attend the Billboard Latin Music Awards

Benito's album had done something very rarely seen, crossing over and finding popularity in many charts without giving up his native Spanish language, Puerto Rican culture, and unique style. He became known as the first "reverse crossover artist," meaning he didn't have to sing or act a different way to gain attention from a wider audience. Though Benito is quick to remind others that he wasn't the first to break barriers, always honoring his idols like Héctor Lavoe, Tego Calderón, Daddy Yankee, and many more Puerto Rican artists throughout history.

And as Benito's fame continued to grow, so did his way of thinking about the world. Since Hurricane María, he began to connect with what it meant to be a Puerto Rican artist in a world that knew very little about his island home. His music reflected his personal growth, expressing his beliefs for women's rights in songs such as

"Solo de Mi," "I Belong to Myself," and showing the love of his birthplace and the people who live there. He wanted Puerto Ricans to be proud of where they were from, too, and have a better life, so he created the Good Bunny Foundation in 2018.

Throughout 2019, Benito performed around the world and released a collaborative album with his friend J Balvin titled *Oasis* that reached number nine on the *Billboard* 200. But as busy as he was, he missed his family and friends in Puerto Rico. Though grateful for the success of his music and growing fans, his career kept him away from home for long periods of time. "Setting foot on the island is really important to me," Benito said in an interview with the *New York Times*. For him, visiting Puerto Rico helped him reconnect with his purpose as an artist by going back to where his love of music began.

Benito returns to Puerto Rico to join protesters in 2019

So he did not hesitate to cut his *X 100PRE* Tour in Europe short and fly back to Puerto Rico to join thousands of protesters demanding the resignation of former governor Ricardo Rosselló. Texts from the governor and his team making scornful remarks about Hurricane María victims, Puerto Rican artist Ricky Martin, and more had been released to the public. Benito participated in the protests, not because he felt an artistic responsibility, but because it was his choice as a Puerto Rican and as a human being.

"I believe that every human being has the duty to have empathy for others, to help others . . . to bring a positive change."

Benito showed the world his complexity and passion, not only in his art but also in his activism. And he still strived for more.

CHAPTER 4
YHLQMDLG and *El Último Tour Del Mundo*

Throughout the rest of 2019, Benito dropped hints for the title of his second solo album, eventually revealed as *YHLQMDLG*, an acronym for *Yo Hago Lo Que Me Da La Gana*, "I Do Whatever I Want," before releasing it on February 29, 2020, just before the world went into lockdown due to the Coronavirus disease, COVID-19. The album debuted at number one on both Top Latin Albums and Latin Rhythm Albums and number two on the US *Billboard* 200, became the highest-charting all-Spanish album on record, and was nominated for Best Latin Pop or Urban Album at the 2021 Grammys.

The album was filled with a playful blend of musical styles on hits like "Si Veo a Tu Mamá," "If I See Your Mom," and "Vete," "Leave." It featured musical guests including reggaeton legends such as Daddy Yankee, Ñengo Flow, and Jowell & Randy. *YHLQMDLG* won the Grammy Award for Best Latin Pop or Urban Album and the Billboard Latin Music Awards for Top Latin Album of the Year and Latin Rhythm Album of the Year. On September 20, 2020, the three-year anniversary of Hurricane María, he performed a free concert in New York City on top of a large truck decorated as a subway car! He sang songs like "La Difícil," "Difficult," and "La Canción," "The Song," with his friend J Balvin, who joined him virtually all the way from Colombia! The truck drove through the Bronx, then through the Manhattan neighborhoods of Washington Heights and Harlem, stopping at the Harlem Hospital Center.

And not even nine months after *YHLQMDLG* came out, Benito released his third album on November 27, 2020, *El Último Tour Del Mundo*, "The Last Tour of the World." The album broke his US *Billboard* 200 record within that same year. For the second time in a year, he'd broken records and expectations, blending rock, reggaeton, and trap, even including a track by Trio Vegabajeño, a Puerto Rican band. He won the American Music Award for Favorite Latin Album and the Latin Grammy Award for Best Urban Music Album.

But even with all his fame and success, Benito's parents remained unfazed. While they don't fully understand the level of his fame, Tito and Lysaurie always support their son. Benito could always count on his family and friends to keep his feet on the ground, escaping the pressure of being Bad Bunny.

He could go to his parents' home, relax,

and feel as if nothing had changed. When Benito went home, he was Benito, not Bad Bunny. For him, it was important to keep his family close, even when he was far away. He still had the same friends he had had since high school—some even worked with him in making music, like Ormani, now a well-known DJ. And sometimes his brothers, Bysael and Bernie, would join him on his tours around the world.

When he was ready to return to the world as Bad Bunny, he was determined to do whatever he wanted, sing whatever he wanted, and wear whatever he wanted.

And in between making three albums, he had been training to make another childhood dream come true.

On January 31, 2021, Benito debuted in the WWE Royal Rumble, allied with Damian Priest to win the WWE 24/7 Championship.

He had trained under Damian, who was impressed by his dedication and love of wrestling, and they would later become close friends.

Performing in the WWE was one of the best days of Benito's life. In an interview with *Time* magazine he said, "It was like I was a kid all over again. And the fight--it was the blink of an eye. Everything happened fast."

But that seemed like Benito's very nature. To try new things, to always improve, and to share his success. And it didn't go unnoticed as *Time* magazine named him one of the Most Influential People of 2021. J Balvin, one of Benito's close friends from the very beginning of their music careers, described Benito as someone who reached superstar status, connected with fans through his amazing lyrics, and championed the importance of being yourself.

31

CHAPTER 5
Un Verano Sin Ti

In 2022, Benito appeared in the hit movie *Bullet Train* with actor Brad Pitt, a moment

he found both overwhelming and inspiring. He even thought the fight scenes in the movie were more difficult than fighting on WWE! Acting was something Benito had always liked but he never had the resources to pursue. His main priority was always his music.

Brad Pitt and Benito in *Bullet Train*

On May 6, 2022, Benito released his fourth solo album, *Un Verano Sin Ti*, "A Summer Without You," breaking his own record on the US *Billboard* 200 by hitting the top of the chart and staying at number one for thirteen weeks.

Un Verano Sin Ti

Much like his previous albums, Benito created this album by tapping into his Caribbean roots and including reggaeton, cumbia, reggae, and salsa. His musical collaborators included artists like Puerto Rican duo Buscabulla, Colombian band Bomba Estéreo, and others.

Un Verano Sin Ti was a blend of his first three albums, with songs about relaxing for vacation like "Me Fui de Vacaciones," "I Went on Vacation," to love songs such as "Ojitos Lindos," "Pretty Eyes." One of his most popular songs titled "El Apagón," "The Blackout," is a tribute to his Puerto Rican roots. It tackled issues Puerto Ricans faced at the time, like the ongoing island-wide blackouts after the Canadian-American company Luma was brought in to operate Puerto Rico's electrical system and increased electricity bills for Puerto Ricans to be more than double the average US rate. They were also faced with gentrification, a process where locals are displaced out of their communities by the rising cost of living. This makes it impossible for them to afford to stay in their own homes. And then wealthier homeowners and renters can easily move in, forever changing the community.

The music video for "El Apagón" celebrates several artists and athletes from Puerto Rico, such as professional boxer Félix "Tito" Trinidad, actor Raul Julia, and Pedro Albizu Campos, a Puerto Rican politician who was a leading figure of the independence movement for Puerto Rico. Immediately following the music video is an eighteen-minute documentary that details the ongoing struggles of Puerto Ricans trying to survive in their homeland. It was made with journalist Bianca Graulau. The video was shortlisted (named to a small group of contenders) along with Spanish singer Rosalía's "Motomami" and Pharrell William's "Cash In Cash Out," for the 2023 Cannes Lion Awards in the Excellence in Music Video Category.

In 2023, *Un Verano Sin Ti* became the most

streamed album on Spotify, a digital music service, making Benito the most streamed artist for over three years. It reached the top ten on charts all over the world, and it was written and performed entirely in Spanish.

But when Benito performed at the Grammys, his lyrics were not translated into English in the captions. The production team for the program included closed captions that said simply "singing in non-English." It was insensitive of the National Academy of Recording Arts and Sciences, the people who produce the Grammys, not to think ahead and have a translator on the team.

"It's ugly to say that I saw it as normal," Benito explained in an interview with *Vanity Fair* magazine. "Why don't they have someone? Knowing that I was going to be there."

But Benito chose not to dwell on the event, staying true to his long-held belief of singing for those who want to listen and to those who understood him. Because even though Benito did whatever he wanted and wrote whatever he wanted, he always wrote for, and about, his birthplace. "I do music for Puerto Rico," he said in an interview. "I'm a fan of our people, our culture." He even made a surprise performance on top of a gas station in San Juan, Puerto Rico, for his fans!

Juggling so many projects, Benito moved to Los Angeles, California, in January 2023 to work on his next album, prepare to tour, and continue to act. He had considered living in other places around the world before ultimately moving back to Puerto Rico for good. To him, Puerto Rico would always be his home. But there was so much more of the world he wanted to experience.

In 2023, Benito was invited to be the first Latino solo act to headline the Coachella festival in Indio, California. His performance was a two-hour-long event with guest performances by Jowell y Randy, Ñengo Flow, and Post Malone. For his show, he wanted to bring *el barrio*, "the neighborhood," to his fans at Coachella in the Southern California desert. He reminded them that he wasn't the first Puerto Rican to break through and change the world—there were many others before him, and many more to come.

In September of that same year, he starred alongside Gael García Bernal in the biographical drama *Cassandro*. And then in true Benito fashion, he released his fifth solo album, *Nadie Sabe Lo Que Va a Pasar Mañana*, "No One Knows What Will Happen Tomorrow," on Friday, October 13.

And it remains true: There is no telling what else Benito will accomplish. Fans are eager to see what other surprises he has in store for them.

At Coachella, 2023

During his Coachella performance, he told his fans, in Spanish, "Sé cuál es mi proposito en la tierra y se los juro que lo voy a cumplir."

"I know what my purpose is on earth and I swear I'll make it come true."

What was the purpose he saw? We can only wait to find out.

43

The Good Bunny Foundation

The Good Bunny Foundation is a nonprofit organization that supports the arts, music, and sports for children in Puerto Rico. The foundation created the summer camp called Un Verano Contigo, "A Summer With You," where kids could play and practice sports, learn music, and create art. The Good Bunny Foundation also partnered with the Maestro Cares Foundation, founded by Puerto Rican singer Marc Anthony, to restore Little League baseball fields across Puerto Rico.

"Growing up on the island, I spent a lot of time in some of these parks that are now destroyed," Benito said. A lot of great athletes like Roberto Clemente, Yadier Molina, Roberto Alomar, Edgar Martínez, and Iván Rodríguez had grown up in parks similar to these. "Our commitment is to rebuild these parks so that we can help new athletes grow."

After Hurricane María, the Good Bunny Foundation helped reconstruct homes and provided free meals. They also hold an annual Bonita Tradición, "Beautiful Tradition," gift drive, giving over twenty thousand presents of instruments, sports equipment, and materials for painting to the children of Puerto Rico. They serve food, play live music, and give kids a chance to take a picture with Los Reyes Magos, "the Three Kings," and even Benito himself.

Timeline of Bad Bunny's Life

1994 — Born Benito Antonio Martínez Ocasio on March 10 in Vega Baja, Puerto Rico

2016 — Publishes his first songs through SoundCloud

— Signs with record label Hear This Music

2018 — Begins the Una Nueva Religión, "A New Religion," Tour

— Releases *X 100PRE*, his debut album, which is listed number forty-one on *Rolling Stone* magazine's list of 100 Best Debut Albums of all time

2019 — Releases *Oasis*, a collaborative album with J Balvin

— Wins Latin Grammy for Best Urban Music Album for *X 100PRE*

2020 — Releases *YHLQMDLG* and becomes the first Spanish-language artist to become Spotify's most-streamed artist globally, with over 8.3 billion streams

— Releases *El Último Tour Del Mundo*, which becomes the first all-Spanish-language album to reach number one on the *Billboard* 200

2021 — Participates in WWE Royal Rumble in Tampa, Florida

2022 — Appears in *Bullet Train*

— Becomes the first Latin artist to be named MTV's Video Music Awards Artist of the Year

2023 — Breaks world record for most streamed album on Spotify

Timeline of the World

1994 — Winter Olympics held in Lillehammer, Norway

2013 — The Supreme Court strikes down federal law defining marriage as between a man and woman, legalizing same-sex marriage

2016 — Cleveland Cavaliers win their first NBA, National Basketball Association, championship

2017 — A total solar eclipse crosses the United States from coast to coast

2018 — American actress Meghan Markle marries the Duke of Sussex Prince Harry, becoming Duchess of Sussex

2019 — Ricardo Rosselló resigns as governor of Puerto Rico amid text scandals

2020 — Global shutdown due to the COVID-19 pandemic

2021 — NASA Rover Perseverance touches down on Mars

2022 — Missing seventeenth-century Spanish galleon *Santo Cristo de Burgos* found off the coast of northern Oregon

2023 — 205th anniversary of Mary Shelley's publication of *Frankenstein*

Bibliography

Chocano, Carina. "The World's Newest Superhero: Bad Bunny."
GQ. May 24, 2022. https://www.gq.com/story/bad-bunny-june-cover-profile.

Chow, Andrew R., and Mariah Espada. "'I Make Music Like I'm the Only Person in the World.' Bad Bunny on Coachella, Hollywood, and Life on Top." *Time*. March 28, 2023. https://time.com/6266336/bad-bunny-interview-coachella/.

del Valle Schorske, Carina. "The World According to Bad Bunny." *New York Times*. October 11, 2020. https://www.nytimes.com/interactive/2020/10/07/magazine/bad-bunny.html.

Exposito, Suzy. "Bad Bunny in Captivity." *Rolling Stone*. May 14, 2020. https://www.rollingstone.com/music/music-features/bad-bunny-cover-story-lockdown-puerto-rico-new-albums-996871/.

Flores, Griselda. "Bad Bunny Spreads Holiday Joy in Puerto Rico with 'Bonita Tradición' Gift Drive." *Billboard*. December 27, 2022. https://www.billboard.com/music/latin/bad-bunny-gift-drive-puerto-rico-good-bunny-foundation-1235191469/.

Guerrero, Jean. "Bad Bunny stays true to himself at Coachella." *Los Angeles Times*. April 21, 2023. https://www.latimes.com/opinion/story/2023-04-21/coachella-bad-bunny-latin-music-politics-puerto-rico.

Lopez, Julyssa. "Bad Bunny Conquered the World. Now What?" *Rolling Stone*. June 21, 2023. https://www.rollingstone.com/music/music-features/bad-bunny-coachella-el-apagon-controversy-future-interview-1234770225/.

Lopez, Julyssa, and Larisha Paul. "Bad Bunny Opens 2023 Grammy Awards With a Proud Ode to Puerto Rico." *Rolling Stone*. February 5, 2023. https://www.rollingstone.com/music/music-latin/bad-bunny-2023-grammys-performance-despues-de-la-playa-1234673176/.

Shaffer, Claire. "Bad Bunny to Perform Live at WWE Royal Rumble." *Rolling Stone*. January 26, 2021. https://www.rollingstone.com/music/music-news/bad-bunny-wwe-royal-rumble-1119136/.